THE UNDERWATER 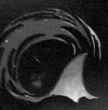 WORLD OF SHARKS™

the WHALE shark

Brad Burnham

The Rosen Publishing Group's
PowerKids Press™
New York

For my mom

Published in 2001 by The Rosen Publishing Group, Inc.
29 East 21st Street, New York, NY 10010

First Edition

Book Design: Maria Melendez

Photo Credits: Cover, title page © CORBIS/Bettmann; pp. 4, 9 © Jeffrey L. Rotman; p. 5 © Stephen Frink; p. 8 © Amos Nachoum; title page, 8, 10, 16 © Digital Stock; title page, 6, 7, 10, 11, 12, 13, 14, 15, 16, 17, 20, 21 © Peter Arnold; pp. 2, 3, 17, 22, 23, 24 © Animals, Animals; pp. 18, 19 © Innerspace Visions.

Burnham, Brad.
   The whale shark / Brad Burnham.—1st ed.
     p. cm.— (The underwater world of sharks)
   Summary: Introduces the physical characteristics, behavior, habitat, and life cycle of the whale shark.
   ISBN 0-8239-5587-7 (alk. paper)
   1. Whale shark—Juvenile literature. [1. Whale shark. 2. Sharks.] I. Title. II. Series.

QL638.95.R4 B87 2000
597.3—dc21
                                                  00-022375

Contents

Not a Whale

Whale sharks are not whales at all. They are fish. In fact whale sharks are the largest fish in the world. Adult whale sharks can be as long as 40 feet (12.2 m) and weigh 20 tons (18.1 tonnes)! Some people have seen whale sharks that could have been more than 50 feet (15.2 m) long. The sharks swam away before they could be measured.

The **species** name of whale sharks is *Rhincodon typus*. The word *"Rhincodon"* means *"***rasp** teeth.*" Whale sharks have many small teeth. Their teeth are like the teeth on a rasp, or file.

Whale sharks are not whales, but fish. In fact they are the largest fish in the ocean.

A Big Checkerboard

Whale sharks are reddish brown in color. They have a pattern of lines on their skin that crisscross each other. The lines form a **grid**. Inside the grid are yellow dots. The whole pattern looks like a big checkerboard.

The pattern of lines and dots on a whale shark's skin might be **camouflage**. Camouflage is a shape or color pattern that helps an animal hide from other animals that want to eat it. Animals that hunt other animals for food are called **predators**. Camouflage protects whale sharks by making them blend in with the rest of the ocean. Adult whale sharks are very large. They do not need to hide from predators. The camouflage pattern might be to help young whale sharks hide from predators.

The whale shark's skin is very rough. It is made up of pointy, sharp, toothlike scales. ▶

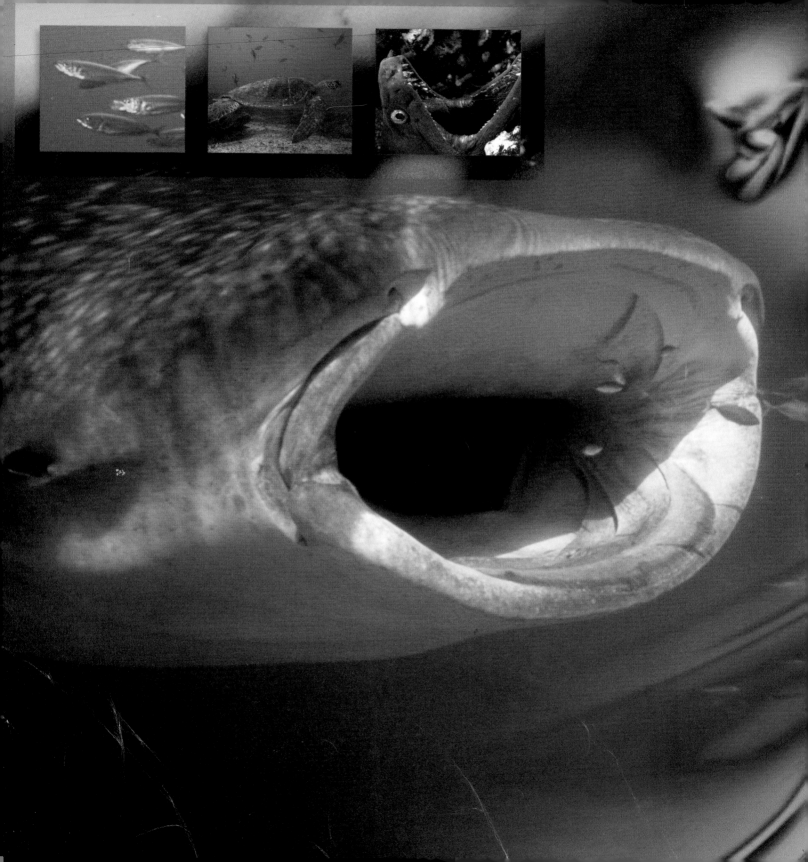

Where Whale Sharks Live

Whale sharks live in the Atlantic, Pacific, and Indian Oceans. They are a **pelagic** species. This means they swim in the open ocean. Whale sharks are usually found in the **tropical** parts of the oceans. Sometimes they do swim into cooler water, though.

There have been more than 100 whale shark sightings by people. Whale sharks have been seen near the surface of the ocean. They have also been seen by the shore. When whale sharks swim into deep parts of the ocean it is to search for **prey**. Prey are animals that are eaten by other animals.

◀ *Whale sharks are a pelagic species. Pelagic species swim in the open ocean.*

9

Tiny Teeth

There are thousands of tiny teeth inside the mouth of a whale shark. There might be as many as 4,000 teeth. Each tooth is only about 1/8 of an inch (.3 cm) high. The teeth are arranged in the mouth in 300 rows. These rows are called **dentary bands**.

Whale sharks do not use their teeth to eat. They have lots of teeth, but the teeth are not big enough to help them catch and eat prey. Scientists do not know why whale sharks have teeth.

You cannot see the whale shark's teeth in this picture. This is because each tooth is about the size of the tip of a match. ▶

How Whale Sharks Breathe

Whale sharks breathe with gills. Gills are **organs** that fish have in their mouths. Whale sharks use their gills to get oxygen from the water. Oxygen is a gas that helps animals breathe. Whale sharks swim with their mouths open. Water enters the mouth and passes over the gills. The gills remove oxygen from the water. The water leaves the mouth through slits in the gills. Whale sharks have five gill slits on each side of their head.

Whale sharks use **gill rakers** to trap food. This helps them filter tiny fish out of the water. The fish get trapped in the gill rakers. After the whale shark eats its food, the food is digested in the shark's stomach.

◀ *Oxygen is removed from the water by a whale shark's gills. The water then leaves the mouth through the gill slits.*

Big Fish, Small Food

Whale sharks are the biggest fish in the world. Still, they eat some of the smallest animals in the ocean. Whale sharks eat plankton. Plankton are plants and animals that float in the water. Most plankton are very small. Whale sharks eat plankton such as krill. Krill are very much like shrimp. Krill are an inch (2.5 cm) or less in size. Whale sharks also eat small fish and squid.

Whale sharks catch the animals they eat by swimming with their mouths open. The mouth of a 35-foot (10.7-m) whale shark is 6 feet (1.8 m) wide. Water and small animals go into the whale shark's mouth as it swims. When the water leaves the whale shark's mouth through the gill slits, the animals get trapped in the gill rakers.

Whale sharks sometimes eat larger fish such as tuna. They also eat plankton such as krill. ▶

Leading the Way

Whale sharks do not swim alone. Smaller fish like to swim with whale sharks. Sometimes whale sharks have a whole **school** of fish swimming around them. Pilot fish swim around the heads of whale sharks. Some scientists believe that by swimming with the sharks, pilot fish are protected. Enemies of pilot fish are probably afraid to come too close.

Remoras also swim with whale sharks. Each remora has a **ridged** sucker on its head. It uses the sucker to attach itself to the whale shark. Remoras sometimes help whale sharks by eating **parasites** off their skin. Parasites can cause harm by living off whale sharks. They live off the sharks and offer nothing in return.

Some fish swim next to whale sharks as protection against enemies.

Giving Birth

Scientists used to think that female whale sharks laid eggs. Now they know that whale sharks keep their eggs inside their bodies until the babies are ready to be born. These babies are called **pups**. A shark might have many eggs inside of her. Not every egg will become an **embryo**. The eggs that do become embryos eat other eggs for energy.

In 1995, a team of scientists found a pregnant whale shark in Taiwan. The whale shark had been killed by a fisherman. There were 300 embryos inside of the whale shark. Fifteen of the embryos were still alive and ready to be born.

Whale shark pups are born perfectly formed. They look just like adult whale sharks except they are smaller. ▶

Giant but Gentle

Whale sharks are large but gentle fish. They eat only plankton and other small fish. They are not interested in eating other things. People are able to swim close to whale sharks. Swimmers even hold onto the fins of a whale shark to get a ride. At Ningaloo Reef, off the northwest coast of Australia, people swim with whale sharks. People visit the reef from March until late April. During this time, whale sharks gather near the reef. Whale sharks pay no attention to boats. Whale sharks and boats have occasionally run into each other. Boat captains need to be careful when they travel in waters where whale sharks swim.

◀ *When whale sharks get tired of people riding on them, they dive deep down into the ocean.*

Good-Luck Fish

Sharks have played different roles in the beliefs of many groups of people. Some people see sharks as troublemakers. Other people think of them as gods. Whale sharks are considered by Japanese fishermen to be a sign of good luck. The fishermen are careful not to catch or harm whale sharks. They call the whale shark *ebisuzame*, which is a good-luck symbol. In Vietnam whale sharks are called "Ca Ong," which means "Sir Fish." Sir Fish is a god that Vietnamese fishermen pray to for protection. They build small shrines to whale sharks on the beaches. It is clear that these huge, gentle fish play an important part in many people's lives.

Glossary

camouflage (KA-muh-flaj) The color or pattern of an animal's feathers, fur, or skin that helps it blend into its surroundings.

dentary bands (DEN-tar-ee BANDZ) The rows of teeth in a shark's mouth.

embryo (EM-bree-oh) A plant or animal in the early stages of its growth.

gill rakers (GIL RAY-kerz) The parts of a whale shark that strain fish out of the water to use for food.

grid (GRID) A pattern of evenly spaced lines running up, down, and across.

organs (OR-genz) Parts of a plant or an animal that do one certain thing.

parasites (PAR-eh-syts) Organisms that live on or in another type of organism and receive nutrients.

pelagic (pe-LAYJ-ik) Living at or near the surface of the open ocean.

predators (PREH-duh-terz) Animals that kill other animals for food.

prey (PRAY) An animal that is eaten by another animal for food.

pups (PUHPS) A type of baby animal.

rasp (RASP) A tool used to file something down.

Rhincodon typus (REEN-ko-don TY-pus) The scientific name for the whale shark.

ridged (RIJD) Covered with raised and narrow strips.

school (SKOOL) A group of fish.

species (SPEE-sheez) A group of living things that have certain basic things in common.

tropical (TRAH-pih-kul) An area that is very hot and humid year-round.

Index

Web Sites

To learn more about whale sharks, check out these Web sites:
http://www.whaleshark.org
http://www.njscuba.com/Eco/WhaleSharks